STECK-VAUGHN

PORTRAIT OF AMERICA

Louisiana

Steck-Vaughn Company

Executive Editor	Diane Sharpe
Senior Editor	Martin S. Saiewitz
Design Manager	Pamela Heaney
Photo Editor	Margie Foster

Proof Positive/Farrowlyne Associates, Inc.
Program Editorial, Revision Development, Design, and Production

Consultant: John T. Parker, President, Convention and Visitors Channel

Published by Raintree Steck-Vaughn Publishers, an imprint of Steck-Vaughn Company.

A Turner Educational Services, Inc. book. Based on the Portrait of America television series by R. E. (Ted) Turner.

Cover Photo: Bourbon Street, New Orleans by © David Ball/The Stock Market.

Library of Congress Cataloging-in-Publication Data

Thompson, Kathleen.
    Louisiana / Kathleen Thompson.
        p. cm. — (Portrait of America)
    "A Turner book."
    "Based on the Portrait of America television series"—T.p. verso.
    Includes index.
    ISBN 0-8114-7338-4 (library binding).—ISBN 0-8114-7443-7 (softcover)
    1. Louisiana—Juvenile literature. I. Title. II. Series:
Thompson, Kathleen. Portrait of America.
F369.3 .T46 1996
976.3—dc20

                        95-22685
                          CIP
                          AC

Printed and Bound in the United States of America

2 3 4 5 6 7 8 9 10 WZ 98 97

Acknowledgments
The publishers wish to thank the following for permission to reproduce photographs:
P. 7 Louisiana Office of Tourism; p. 8 © D. Donne Bryant; p. 10 New Orleans Museum of Art: Gift of William E. Groves; p. 11 Chicago Historical Society; p. 12 Library of Congress; p. 13 Louisiana Office of Tourism; pp. 14, 15 North Wind Picture Archives; p. 16 New Orleans Mayor's Office; p. 17 Reuters/Bettmann; p. 18 UPI/Bettmann; p. 19 Hill Memorial Library, Louisiana State University; pp. 20, 21 UPI/Bettmann; p. 22 © D. Donne Bryant; p. 23 © B. A. Cohen; p. 24 Louisiana Office of Tourism; p. 25 © B. A. Cohen; p. 26 Lafayette Convention and Visitors Commission; p. 28 Louisiana Office of Tourism; p. 29 American Sugar Cane League/Sides and Associates; p. 30 Louisiana Office of Tourism; p. 31 (top) U. S. Department of the Interior, Fish and Wildlife Service, (bottom) Louisiana Office of Tourism; p. 32 © D. Donne Bryant; p. 33 Courtesy Shell Offshore, Incorporated; p. 35 Lafayette Convention and Visitors Commission; p. 36 Louisiana Office of Tourism; p. 37 (top) Steven Spencer/Louisiana Office of Tourism, (bottom) Hogan Jazz Archive, Howard–Tilton Memorial Library, Tulane University; p. 38 (top) Shreveport Tourism, (bottom) Louisiana Office of Tourism; p. 39 The Bettmann Archive; p. 40 © D. Donne Bryant; p. 41 UPI/Bettmann; p. 42 © Superstock; p. 44 Louisiana Office of Tourism; p. 46 One Mile Up; p. 47 (top) Louisiana Office of Tourism, (bottom) One Mile Up.

STECK-VAUGHN

PORTRAIT OF AMERICA

Louisiana

Kathleen Thompson

A Turner Book

RSVP

RAINTREE
STECK-VAUGHN
P U B L I S H E R S
The Steck-Vaughn Company

Austin, Texas

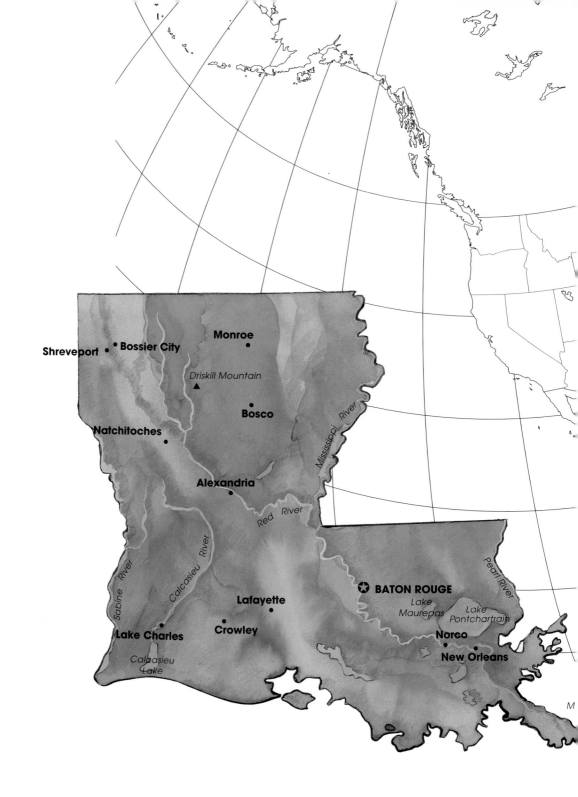

Louisiana

Shreveport • • Bossier City

Monroe •

Driskill Mountain ▲

Bosco

Natchitoches •

Alexandria •

Red River

Sabine River

Calcasieu River

Mississippi River

Lafayette •

Crowley •

Lake Charles •

Calcasieu Lake

★ BATON ROUGE

Lake Maurepas

Lake Pontchartrain

Pearl River

Norco •

New Orleans •

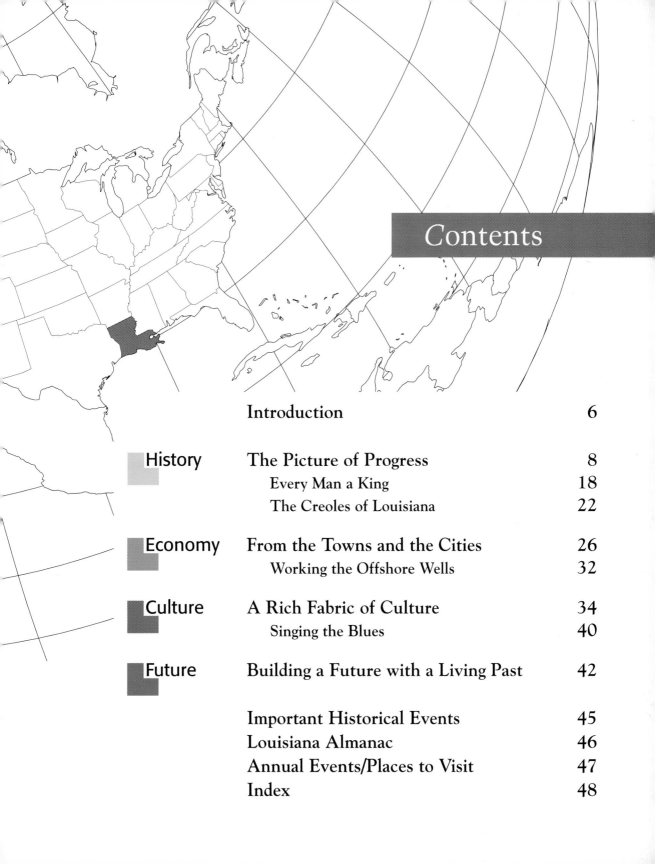

Contents

Introduction

The people of Louisiana love to eat gumbo, a tasty cross between a soup and a stew. Like gumbo, the state's culture is a spicy mixture of Europe, Africa, and America, with an accent all its own. Louisiana's northern region was settled by north Europeans. As the state stretches south toward the mouth of the Mississippi River, it picks up the zesty flavor of French and Spanish traditions. People of African descent add spice throughout the state. Louisiana's cultural gumbo reaches its peak in the city of New Orleans, one of the world's busiest seaports. Here, modern business and industry thrive in Old World surroundings to the African-born sounds of jazz, America's great gift to music.

Cypress trees, such as these in Chicot Cajun Country State Park, enjoy the warm southern climate.

Louisiana

ajuns, crawfish, cotton, oil wells

The Picture of Progress

The great Mississippi River flows south, through plains and farmland, to the Gulf of Mexico. And there, where it spills into the gulf, are the bayous of the land we now call Louisiana. There is evidence of Native Americans living in the area as far back as 16,000 years ago. Most lived as hunters and gatherers. Those who made their home in the southern portion of the state were also farmers. There were about 15,000 Native Americans living in various villages throughout the area. They belonged to about thirty groups, including the Tunica, Caddo, Atakapa, and the Chitimacha.

Alvarez de Pineda, a Spanish explorer, reached the mouth of the Mississippi River in 1519 while sailing along the Gulf of Mexico. It was his expedition that proved to the Spanish that the "island" of La Florida was much more than an island. In 1539 Hernando de Soto began an expedition from the coast of Florida. Two years later, the expedition reached the Mississippi River, which de Soto claimed for Spain. A year later, de Soto died. He was buried in the Mississippi.

The Cabildo was constructed in 1795 as the seat of the Spanish government in New Orleans. It now serves as the main building of the Louisiana State Museum historical museum complex.

This nineteenth century painting shows Louisiana Native Americans walking along a bayou.

The French also explored this area. In 1682 René-Robert Cavelier, Sieur de La Salle, canoed down the Mississippi with the help of Henry de Tonti, a French explorer and trader. At the mouth of the river, La Salle claimed all of the land around the Mississippi for France and named it Louisiana in honor of the king of France, Louis XIV. So the area the French called Louisiana was a much larger area than today's state.

Although the Spanish were the first Europeans to explore the region, it was the French who settled the area. Seventeen years after La Salle's expedition, French settlers began to arrive to colonize the area. Pierre Le Moyne, Sieur d'Iberville, and his brother founded permanent colonies. D'Iberville made his home at what is now Ocean Springs, Mississippi. It became the capital of the colony of Louisiana. His brother, Jean-Baptiste Le Moyne de Bienville, founded New Orleans in 1718.

In 1702 the capital of the Louisiana colony moved from Ocean Springs to Fort Louis de la Mobile. This area is near present-day Mobile, Alabama. In 1722 the capital moved again, this time to New Orleans.

In the meantime, traders had become important to Louisiana. First, in 1712, France gave exclusive trading rights in the colony to a merchant named Antoine Crozat. Louisiana was still French, but it was not a royal colony anymore. It was a proprietary colony, controlled by Crozat. He intended to put money into the colony and take profits out. It was a business deal. But it was a deal that didn't work, and Crozat lost a lot of money. In 1717 he gave up his trading rights. The colony was given to a company run by a Scottish man, John Law. By 1720 John Law's plans to develop the colony had failed, too. The Louisiana colony became a royal colony again in 1731.

This lithograph from the early nineteenth century shows La Salle taking possession of Louisiana.

However, the royal colony just wasn't making enough money. So, in 1762, the French government secretly gave the Isle of Orleans and the rest of Louisiana west of the Mississippi River to Spain. This part of the colony included nearly all of the area that was to become the state of Louisiana.

During the 1760s a terrible thing was happening in Canada. Nova Scotia, on the eastern coast of Canada, had been settled by both British and French people. But then the British took over the area. They forced out a whole group of French people who lived in an area of Nova Scotia called Acadia. Suddenly the Acadians were homeless. Many of the Acadians came south to Louisiana to be with other French people. Over the years, Acadia came to be pronounced *Cajun*, and that is what many of the people of Louisiana are called today.

New Orleans was a busy seaport in 1873.

The Oak Alley Plantation in Vacherie shows the wealth of some plantation owners before the Civil War.

The colony grew to a population of fifty thousand under the able leadership of several Spanish governors. Bernardo de Gálvez became governor during the American Revolution. When Spain declared war on Great Britain in 1779, Gálvez opened the port of New Orleans to American ships and sold them supplies. He also led Spanish forces in the capture of British forts along the lower Mississippi and the Gulf of Mexico, including Baton Rouge, Mobile, and Pensacola.

In 1800 Spain returned Louisiana to France. The French government sold the area to the United States. The sale was called the Louisiana Purchase. For $15 million, the United States bought all of Louisiana. The area included all of the Mississippi Valley region, stretching to the Canadian border. The Louisiana Purchase doubled the size of the United States.

In 1804 Congress divided the huge area into two territories. The part called the Territory of Louisiana included the larger area of the Mississippi Valley. The part that is now the state of Louisiana was called the Territory of Orleans. The Territory of Orleans was divided into 19 parishes. No other state is divided into parishes instead of counties. The term *parish* dates back to when the Spanish ruled.

On April 30, 1812, the Territory of Orleans became the state of Louisiana, the eighteenth state to join the Union. New Orleans was its capital, and William C.C. Claiborne was its first governor.

A major battle of the War of 1812 between the United States and Great Britain was fought in New Orleans. The British began to attack the city at about the same time a peace treaty was being written.

The Battle of New Orleans was the last major battle of the War of 1812.

Neither army, of course, knew about this development. On January 8, 1815, the British attacked Andrew Jackson's army. In a short time the British force had been destroyed. More than 1,500 British soldiers were killed or wounded. Fourteen American soldiers were killed and about 39 were wounded.

Louisiana thrived in the years leading to the Civil War. More and more people settled in the state. By 1860 the state's population had grown to over seven hundred thousand. About half of these people were slaves. Sugar cane and cotton plantations flourished. And with the invention of the railroad and the river steamboat, businesses could move goods faster, farther, and cheaper than before. Louisiana was rapidly becoming an important center of world trade.

In 1861 Louisiana withdrew from the Union and prepared for the Civil War. Louisiana sent many soldiers and supplies into battle. The Union Navy took control of the ports of New Orleans and Baton Rouge in 1862. This action closed the mouth of the Mississippi River to the Confederacy. Union forces controlled all of the Mississippi after Vicksburg, and Port Hudson surrendered in July 1863.

The time after the war—Reconstruction—was a very difficult time for Louisiana, as it was for the other southern states. Before he died Abraham Lincoln had pleaded for kindness and understanding toward southern people who had fought in the Civil War. After his death it was not kindness, but an angry justice, that ruled the country. People—and states—were punished for being part of the Confederacy.

Andrew Jackson's victory at New Orleans made him a national folk hero.

Louisiana was taken back fully into the Union in 1868. But a political conflict occurred. Members of the Union government fought with those who wished to remain Confederates. The Louisiana government remained unsettled for a number of years. Because of this, federal troops remained in the state until 1877.

Louisiana then worked to improve its economy. The first industries started were processing plants for rice, sugar cane, and cotton. Lumber companies took advantage of the state's dense forests. The discovery of oil and gas reserves also helped develop the state's economy.

In the 1920s a colorful and interesting man became a part of Louisiana politics. His name was Huey P. Long. Much has been written about Huey Long. Some people thought he was a dangerous man. Others saw him as the savior of the poor people of the state. Everyone agreed that he was important.

Huey Long was elected governor of Louisiana in 1928. He built highways, bridges, and schools. He developed social welfare programs and gave free textbooks to schoolchildren. Some people disliked him because they felt he had too much power. Some people thought he was a dishonest politician. Huey Long was elected to the United States Senate in 1930. He was shot to death inside the Louisiana State Capitol in 1935.

Industry continued to grow in Louisiana during and after World War II. Louisiana expanded its oil and gas production to include offshore oil drilling in the Gulf of Mexico. People moved to the cities to work in the factories.

Hurricane Andrew blew across New Orleans in August 1992. Overturned and partially damaged trailers sit in this flooded trailer park in Bayou Vista.

In the 1950s and 1960s, there were racial problems all over the United States. Louisiana was no exception. Hundreds of years of injustice and inequality began to give way to change. The graduate school at Louisiana State University admitted African American students for the first time in 1950. Louisiana elementary schools were open to all races in 1960. Other public buildings became integrated in following years.

Ernest N. "Dutch" Morial of New Orleans was elected to the Louisiana House of Representatives in 1968. He was the first African American to be elected to that office since Reconstruction. He became the first African American mayor of New Orleans in 1977. His son Mark Morial was elected mayor of New Orleans in 1994.

In 1992 Louisiana was hit by Hurricane Andrew, which may have been the worst natural disaster in United States history. The storm caused much greater damage in Florida before crossing the Gulf of Mexico to strike the Louisiana coast. It killed 11 people and caused $1 billion in damage in the state.

Louisiana has learned how to change with the times. Today more people in Louisiana work in factories than on farms. But Louisiana is still a place where the past is alive. Its history is very much a part of its culture.

Every Man a King

Huey P. Long was a remarkable man whose impact on Louisiana is still felt today. He developed a special relationship with a large part of the state's population.

Huey Long knew how to make people laugh. And he knew how to get people to elect him to office. He was a con artist, a wheeler-dealer . . . or the salvation of the people of Louisiana, depending on whom you talk to. His sister Lucille saw many sides of him.

"Nobody ever knew who the governor was until Huey was the governor. Nobody in the United States knew anything about Louisiana—they'd heard of New Orleans—until Huey got to be governor. Huey put Louisiana on the map."

He did that. By the time Huey Long made it to the governor's mansion, everyone in the country had heard of Louisiana—and Huey Long.

Huey Long built his campaign for governor on promises to help the little

Huey Long gestures during a campaign speech.

Huey Long (left) stands along with siblings Lucille and Earl.

people. He spoke of taking from the rich to make "every man a king." He called his plan "Share the Wealth." To finance the plan, Huey Long wanted to set a one hundred percent tax on anyone earning more than one million dollars a year. By 1935 Governor Long claimed to have founded 27,000 Share the Wealth clubs, with a mailing list of over seven million people. The list, he claimed, included workers, farmers, college professors, and even bank presidents.

He ruled Louisiana with an iron hand. Governor Long and his backers were accused of all kinds of corruption, but Huey laughed his way out of it all. His theory was that the people of Louisiana didn't want a good man for governor. They just wanted someone honest enough to admit he was dishonest. They wanted someone who would give them the schools, roads, and hospitals they needed.

And Huey did give these things to the people, as his sister recalled. "He

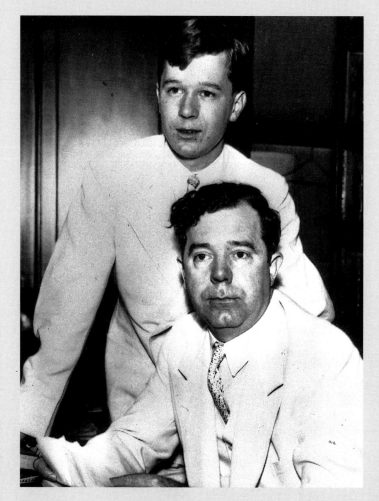

Huey Long was a strong influence on his son Russell, who later became a United States senator.

there and he was telling all these things, you know. And she said—she turned to a friend of hers and she said—'That's the biggest lie that ever was. We never picked any cotton in our life.' And there's an old woman sitting there back behind and she says, 'I bet you did, too.' 'Cause he could make 'em believe anything."

But not everybody believed Huey Long. And not everybody laughed. There were many people in Louisiana, and in other parts of the country, who were afraid of him.

Huey Long wanted to be President of the United States. And many people believed that he could laugh and sell his way into the highest office in our land. If he was dictator of Louisiana,

was elected in 1928. You know he was assassinated in '35. So he only had seven years there. And he built all those bridges. He built the capitol. He built all this highway all over Louisiana."

His brother remembered the faith that the people of Louisiana had in Huey Long. "I know one time he was making a speech and my sister was what would happen if he were ever elected President?

One of the people who feared Huey Long's power, and his ability to misuse it, shot Long to death in the state capitol building in 1935.

Huey's brother Earl carried on the family tradition. In 1939, and again in 1948 and 1956, Earl Long was elected governor of Louisiana. Later, Huey's son Russell was elected to the United States Senate.

Governor Earl Long (left) in New Orleans on a campaign trip in 1959.

The Creoles of Louisiana

Have you ever tasted a special kind of candy called a praline? This sweet blend of nuts and sugar was invented by one of the most interesting cultures in the United States, the Creoles.

Before the Civil War, Creoles were a French-speaking people whose

The French Quarter is one of the oldest sections of New Orleans.

Clementine Hunter is a well-known Creole painter.

ancestors were early French and Spanish settlers. The term *Creole* comes from the Spanish word *criollo*, which means "native to the place." The Creoles lived mainly in southern Louisiana, but many also lived in parts of Alabama and Missouri.

In the days before the Civil War, Louisiana's laws allowed slaves to buy their freedom. These freed people lived in society on a more or less equal basis with other people. As time went by, many of these freed people married into Creole families.

One of the centers of Creole life today is in the Cane River area at Natchitoches. Joe Moran is a member of this community. He talked about the Creoles who call this area home. "Everybody here is related in a way, you know, because just about every person on Cane River can trace his roots back to one man. And this is Augustin Metoyer, who was the son of a free slave woman named Marie Therese who founded the plantation Melrose, which is here on Cane River."

"I really respect the fact that a woman was so instrumental in getting Melrose off the ground, especially a woman who was black and who was a slave," Joe Moran added. ". . . she worked against such odds in that period of time—which was pre-Civil War—to work hard enough to buy her freedom and then also . . . to buy the freedom of all of her children."

This photo shows the quiet beauty of the Cane River area.

Marie Therese's children, grand-children, and great-grandchildren have lived in the Cane River area for well over one hundred years. Joe Moran explained what Cane River means to the people who live there. "There's no other community in America where people who do have African roots have an actual geographical area that they can call home. . . . Every living thing around here embodies this mystery, this ancient air, so to speak."

The Creoles are proud of the past and their heritage, but they have their own special culture. Their mix of ethnic backgrounds is just part of what makes the Creole culture a rich one.

For example, in New Orleans on November 1, All Saints Day is a city-wide holiday. Many people share the Creole tradition of going to a cemetery in family groups to honor the dead. Creole cooking, a blend of Spanish,

French, African, and Native American dishes, remains popular.

The influence of the Creoles is found throughout Louisiana. You can see it in some of the area's finest architecture. You can feel it in the hand-made arts and crafts of the area. You can taste it in the pralines and the rich, hearty soup known as gumbo. In Louisiana, the Creoles have made their mark in many ways.

Doll designer Lair Lacour's Creole Ma-man doll was the official bicentennial doll of Louisiana.

From the Towns and the Cities

As the Mississippi River nears the Gulf of Mexico, its waters branch into smaller and smaller rivers and streams. The delta is veined, like a leaf, with bayous—slow-moving fingers of water leading to and from Louisiana rivers. The air in southern Louisiana is heavy with water, the trees draped with Spanish moss.

When most people think of Louisiana, they have a picture of this lovely, semitropical world at the mouth of the Mississippi River. Or perhaps they think of Mardi Gras, the New Orleans celebration famous for its costumed partygoers and elaborate parades. This is all a part of Louisiana. But there is another side to life in the state today.

Louisiana has long been known for its oil wells and its cotton and sugar cane plantations. However, service industries now account for about 64 percent of the total value of goods and services produced in Louisiana. The leading services include hospitals, hotels, law firms, and repair shops. Wholesale and

Mardi Gras, which means "Fat Tuesday" in French, was introduced to America by the French in the early 1700s.

Louisiana forests, such as the Kisatchie National Forest, are important sources for the state's lumber industry.

retail trade, finance, insurance, and real estate services are also very important to the state's economy.

You might be surprised to find that Louisiana is the third largest oil-producer in the United States. Louisiana has more than 23,000 oil wells. Some are offshore wells in the Gulf of Mexico. About three fourths of Louisiana's wells are in northern Louisiana. The rest are located in the southern part of the state. Near the wells there is natural gas. Louisiana is the second-largest producer of natural gas in the United States. Lake Charles, Norco, and Baton Rouge all have big petroleum refineries.

There are many minerals in the state. Louisiana ranks second only to Texas in value of mineral production. It also ranks second to Texas in the production of sulfur. Louisiana also produces salt, sand, gravel, lignite, and stone.

Although mineral production is very important to the economy of Louisiana, the state is moving away from its dependence on oil and natural gas as it shifts to an economy based on service industries. Mineral production now accounts for only 15 percent of the total value of goods produced in Louisiana.

Manufacturing accounts for about 17 percent of the state's economy. Chemicals are produced in Baton Rouge, Lake Charles, New Orleans, and Shreveport.

Goods made from chemicals include drugs, fertilizer, soap, paint, and plastics. Manufacturing of transportation equipment and paper products are also important to Louisiana's economy.

An industry that is directly linked to Louisiana's natural resources is wood processing. In fact, trees are Louisiana's number one crop. Louisiana has about 15 million acres of commercial timber, covering about 48 percent of its land area. The state's sawmills cut about one billion board feet of lumber each year.

Agriculture is a smaller industry in Louisiana, but the production of Louisiana's farms is important and varied. Soybeans are the most valuable crop. They account for a major portion of the state's cash farm income. But sugar is a big crop, too. Louisiana's sugar industry started in 1795 when Jean Étienne de Boré found a way to process sugar. Today Louisiana is second in the nation in sugar cane production. Twelve percent of the nation's sugar is produced here. Louisiana is third in the United States in rice production. Crowley is called the Rice Capital of Louisiana because of its rice mills.

Louisiana farmers grow more sweet potatoes than farmers do in any state other than North Carolina. Here they're called Louisiana yams. Other crops include corn, grain sorghum, oats, and wheat. Fruit crops produced are strawberries, citrus fruits, peaches, and blueberries. Another important crop is white potatoes. They can be harvested quickly, allowing the farmers to plant a second, different crop in the same fields in the same year.

Today sugar cane is one of Louisiana's most important crops.

Poultry ranks first in animal production. Beef and dairy cattle rank second as a source of farm income in Louisiana. Other livestock farming products include eggs and hogs. The truck farms in southern Louisiana help supply vegetables to states farther north in the winter and spring.

Louisiana is a leading provider of fishery products, such as shrimp, blue crab, and yellowfin tuna. It is also the nation's leading producer of aquaculture livestock. These include crawfish, oysters, catfish, and alligators, which are raised in ponds throughout the state.

Louisiana tourism takes us again to the image of Mardi Gras and Spanish moss. Millions of tourists travel to Louisiana every year for Mardi Gras and to visit New Orleans' beautiful old French and Spanish sections. They sample the delicious food of the Creole and Cajun cultures. They hear New Orleans jazz in the nightclubs and, sometimes, in the streets of the city. They also travel out into the countryside to see the bayous, the small towns, and whitewashed cemeteries. Louisiana, for all its oil wells, is still a place where you can visit the past.

This shrimp boat is ready for another workday.

The 97-acre Natchitoches National Fish Hatchery raises freshwater fish for restocking lakes, rivers, and streams throughout the Gulf Coast region.

Every year millions of tourists visit New Orleans.

Working the Offshore Wells

Oil is becoming less important to Louisiana's economy. However, the oil industry still provides jobs for many people. Most of the oil produced now comes from offshore wells. They are much more expensive and dangerous than land wells.

An offshore well's equipment and workers must be brought there by ship or helicopter. This is one reason offshore drilling costs ten times more than land drilling. Offshore drillers face daily risks such as swinging on ropes and jumping over deep water from a moving boat.

Why do oil companies bother with wells that are so dangerous and expensive? They don't have much choice. Supplies of oil on land are drying up.

Louisiana's first offshore wells were built between 1947 and 1957. Since then, three main types of wells have been developed to explore for oil. Jack-up wells stay closest to the shore. Boats tow these floating wells to areas that might have oil. Then the well's legs are lowered to the ocean floor, jacking the platform above the surface. Another type of well operates partly underwater. These wells explore depths of up to four thousand feet. They are held in place with anchors. The deepest waters, up to eight thousand feet, are explored by drillships. They are the most expensive way to find offshore oil.

So what's it like to work on a Louisiana oil well? Christine Kidder worked on jack-up wells near the

Oil workers repair an oil-drilling platform.

Most jack-up oil wells are used in water depths up to two hundred feet.

coast. She was one of the first women to work the offshore wells. It's an interesting life, but not an easy one.

"Always behind you is the pressure to produce," said Christine. "So each minute that you are having a problem and you're shut in, that's lost production. So the pressure is there, which adds to the challenge. You want to make the best you can. So the ultimate goal is getting it out of the ground and down the pipeline."

Louisiana's oil industry depends on the dedication of its workers. Those like Christine Kidder are willing to take the risks of working on offshore wells.

A Rich Fabric of Culture

In a church basement, a group of women is seated around a quilting frame. Their hands move skillfully across the surface, making the small stitches women have made for generations. On the frame is a patchwork quilt. One piece of fabric is a scrap from a wedding dress. Another is a bit left over from the bright summer dresses a mother made for her twins. There are a hundred colors in the patchwork, a dozen shapes. And it all goes together to make one thing of beauty.

Those women at the quilting frame are a part of Louisiana culture. And their patchwork quilt is as good a symbol as you could find for life in Louisiana. The culture of the state comes from many different sources.

From the plantations came the songs of the slaves, the music of strength and heartache—the blues. The blues moved into the cities, into New Orleans. A brass horn, an upright piano, and a bass changed the rhythm and the sound, and jazz was born.

These musicians play zydeco, a popular musical style in Louisiana.

Floats such as these are a traditional part of the Mardi Gras festivities.

Legendary New Orleans musicians such as King Oliver, Louis Armstrong, and Jelly Roll Morton took the sound of jazz north to Chicago. From there it traveled around the world. Jazz is one of America's most important original art forms, and one of its most popular. The New Orleans jazz tradition continues with musicians such as the Marsalis brothers, Wynton and Branford, who have taken their places among the stars of the jazz world.

From Creole country came another beat—zydeco. Zydeco is a popular music that comes from the Cajun and Creole cultures of the Louisiana bayous. It has a driving rhythm that combines traditional Cajun music with blues and rock. Zydeco is sung in French and uses an accordion as its central instrument.

Wherever you go in the state, there are the sounds of different cultures, the music of different peoples. It's a richness hard to find anywhere else in the world. Here it's a part of life. Music is for work, for parties, for funerals, and for parades.

The people of Louisiana like to celebrate. Whether it's Mardi Gras in New Orleans or a wedding in Cajun country, the celebration

The Breaux Bridge Crawfish Fest is an annual event in Louisiana.

This is a photograph from the early 1920s of King Oliver's Creole Jazz Band.

Crawfish are a common
ingredient in Creole and
Cajun cooking.

The Barnell Garden and Art Center expresses the colorful culture of Louisiana.

usually includes food. Creole and Cajun cooking are famous all over the world. The ingredients are rich and varied. For example, Creole and Cajun cooking use many kinds of peppers, especially hot ones! Onion, garlic, okra, paprika, and cumin are also used. The combinations are unusual and creative. What the people of Louisiana haven't done with a crawfish just can't be done.

The patchwork culture found in Louisiana includes the splendid architecture of the Spanish and French settlers. It is brought out in the imaginations of writers such as Tennessee Williams and Robert Penn Warren. Every stitched-together section is a celebration of life, and the pieces are never quite separate from each other. They blend with each other and move together out of the rich fabric of the past.

Writer Tennessee Williams won two Pulitzer Prizes for works set in Louisiana.

39

Singing the Blues

In the early days of this country, Africans were brought in ships across the ocean. Traders sold them to plantation owners to work in the fields, far from their homes and the lives they had once known. Wives were sold away from husbands. Children were sold away from parents. Even after the Civil War, most African Americans worked in the cotton fields. Their lives were hard, harder than most of us can imagine.

But the people found ways to survive. They took their sorrow and their anger and turned it into something they could use. They took their blues and sang them. They sang the

blues while they worked so they could keep working. They sang the blues so they could keep going.

Clifford Blake once worked in the Louisiana cotton fields. He sang the blues while he worked, both to express his feelings and to provide a rhythm for himself and his fellow workers. For him, "The blues come from a groan. Why, you may be going along the road

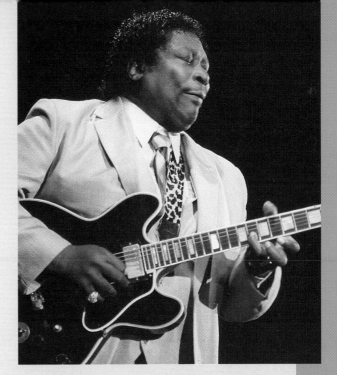

B. B. King is a modern-day blues musician known for his unique guitar-playing style.

This photo shows old slave quarters in Laurel Valley, Louisiana. The hard lives of slaves led to the music known as the blues.

and you don't know what you groaning about. But you done got a little hum inside, inside of your mind. It's down here. You can feel it. It's coming up, but it starts from way down in the center of your stomach."

The blues were a new kind of music—part shout, part cry, part song. They were the roots of almost every kind of American music, from jazz to rock and roll to gospel.

Today in Louisiana the blues are very much alive. In the words of an Irish poet, out of the suffering of the people, "a terrible beauty is born."

41

Building a Future with a Living Past

It's a strange thing about Louisiana. When you look at this fascinating state with its many rich cultures, you just don't seem to worry about the past getting lost. What makes that strange is that Louisiana is very much a part of the world of today.

About two thirds of the state's population now lives in urban areas, and that figure is growing. Mining, manufacturing, and service industries together account for 93 percent of the value of goods produced in the state. That's a figure that makes you think the whole state must be covered with factories and office buildings.

But it's not true. Forests cover about half the state. There are about 1.3 million acres of wildlife-refuge areas. There are three hundred different kinds of birds in Louisiana, and about half of the migrating birds in North America spend the winter in Louisiana.

The Michoud Assembly Facility, which makes equipment for NASA, is in New Orleans. And so is the Louisiana Superdome, a domed sports complex. But it's impossible even to imagine New Orleans

The Superdome in New Orleans is the world's largest indoor arena.

Exotic birds, such as these snowy egrets, were faced with extinction until recent laws made hunting these birds illegal.

without the lacy wrought iron of the French Quarter or the jazz funerals or the Creole cooking.

Louisiana is not, and never has been, a melting pot of cultures. Its rich traditions remain separate, but all of these together make Louisiana a state with a living past. It is a place where you can find chemical plants as well as slow boats on the bayous.

It's easy to think of the high-tech facilities, the factories, and the Superdome as the future. It's easy to place fishing for crawfish in the past. And maybe in some places that would be true. In Louisiana, though, the varied cultures move through time. They are a part, not of history, but of the lives of the people.

Important Historical Events

1541 Hernando de Soto, searching for gold, explores the lower Mississippi River area.

1682 The French explorer René-Robert Cavelier, Sieur de La Salle, claims the Mississippi Valley for France. He names the area Louisiana.

1699 Louisiana becomes a royal colony of France. Pierre le Moyne, Sieur d'Iberville, founds a settlement at what is now Ocean Springs, Mississippi. It is the capital until 1702.

1714 A settlement is founded at present-day Natchitoches. It is the first permanent town in Louisiana.

1718 Jean Baptiste le Moyne, Sieur de Bienville, founds New Orleans, naming it for the Duke of Orleans.

1760 Acadians begin arriving from Nova Scotia.

1762 France gives all of Louisiana west of the Mississippi River plus the Isle of Orleans to Spain.

1779 to 1781 Bernardo de Galvez, Spanish governor of Louisiana, fights the British during the Revolutionary War.

1795 Jean Étienne de Boré develops a method for processing sugar cane into granulated sugar.

1800 Spain gives Louisiana back to France.

1803 The United States purchases Louisiana from France for $15 million.

1804 The Territory of Orleans is created by Congress.

1812 Louisiana becomes the 18th state on April 30. The capital is New Orleans. The governor is William C. C. Claiborne.

1815 Andrew Jackson defeats the British at New Orleans.

1835 Captain Henry M. Shreve founds Shreveport.

1861 Louisiana secedes from the Union.

1862 Union soldiers take New Orleans.

1868 Louisiana is readmitted to the Union.

1877 President Hayes withdraws troops from Louisiana, ending Reconstruction there.

1879 The mouth of the Mississippi River is deepened, so that large ocean ships can reach New Orleans.

1901 Oil is discovered near White Castle and Jennings.

1928 Huey P. Long, born in 1893 near Winnfield, is elected governor.

1935 Huey Long is assassinated.

1958 The longest cantilever bridge in the United States at the time is completed across the Mississippi River at New Orleans.

1964 For the first time since Reconstruction, two Republicans are elected to the Louisiana state legislature.

1965 Hurricane Betsy kills 74 persons.

1975 A new state Constitution goes into effect. The Louisiana Superdome opens in New Orleans.

1984 The World's Fair is held in New Orleans.

1992 Hurricane Andrew kills 11 people and causes one billion dollars in damage.

45

The flag shows a pelican, the state bird, feeding three young pelicans. This symbolizes the state as the provider and protector of its people. The state motto, Union, Justice, and Confidence, appears underneath.

Louisiana Almanac

Nickname. The Pelican State

Capital. Baton Rouge

State Bird. Brown pelican

State Flower. Magnolia

State Tree. Bald cypress

State Motto. Union, Justice, and Confidence

State Song. "Give Me Louisiana"

State Abbreviations. La. (traditional); LA (postal)

Statehood. April 30, 1812, the 18th state

Government. Congress: U.S. senators, 2; U.S. representatives, 7. State Legislature: senators, 39; representatives, 105. Parishes (counties): 64.

Area. 47,720 sq mi (123,593 sq km), 31st in size among the states.

Greatest Distances. north/south, 283 mi (455 km); east/west, 315 mi (507 km). Coastline: 397 mi (639 km)

Elevation. Highest: Driskell Mountain, 535 ft (163 m) above sea level. Lowest: 5 ft (1.5 m) below sea level at New Orleans

Population. 1990 Census: 4,238,216 (.77% increase over 1980), 21st among the states. Density: 89 persons per sq mi (34 persons per sq km). Distribution: 69% urban, 31% rural. 1980 Census: 4,206,098

Economy. *Agriculture:* soybeans, beef cattle, cotton, milk, sugar cane, corn. *Fishing Industry:* shrimp, blue crab, oysters, crawfish. *Fur Industry:* nutria, muskrat. *Manufacturing:* chemicals, petroleum products, transportation equipment, paper products, food products. *Mining:* natural gas, petroleum, salt, sulfur, sand and gravel, stone

State Bird: Brown pelican

State Flower: Magnolia

Annual Events

★ Sugar Bowl football game in New Orleans (New Year's Day)

★ Mardi Gras celebrations (February)

★ Audubon Pilgrimage in St. Francisville (March)

★ New Orleans Spring Fiesta (April)

★ New Orleans Jazz and Heritage Festival (May)

★ Crawfish Festival in Breaux Bridge (May)

★ Louisiana Shrimp and Petroleum Festival in Morgan City (September)

★ Louisiana Cotton Festival in Ville Platte (October)

★ Louisiana State Fair in Shreveport (October)

Places to Visit

★ Audubon Park in New Orleans

★ Avery Island near New Iberia

★ Garden District in New Orleans

★ Grand Isle State Park

★ Jean Lafitte National Historical Park and Preserve in Chalmette

★ Louisiana State Exhibit Museum in Shreveport

★ Natchitoches Country

★ Old State Capitol in Baton Rouge

State Seal

Index